SELKIRKSHIRE
IN OLD PHOTOGRAPHS
FROM THE CLAPPERTON STUDIOS

MERCER'S COACH, seen here leaving Selkirk Market Place, was one which the proprietor of the County Hotel used for a visitors' coach tour to Selkirk and the valleys. The 'Flower of Yarrow' plied the Yarrow valley and connected with the 'Ettrick Shepherd' coach to continue the journey to Moffat.

SELKIRKSHIRE
IN OLD PHOTOGRAPHS
FROM THE CLAPPERTON STUDIOS

—————— COMPILED BY ——————
IAN W. MITCHELL

ALAN SUTTON
1989

Alan Sutton Publishing
Gloucester

First published 1989

British Library Cataloguing in Publication Data

Selkirkshire in old photographs.
1. Scotland. Borders region. Ettrick and
Lauderdale (District), history
I. Mitchell, Ian
941.3'85

ISBN 0-86299-687-2

Typesetting and origination by
Alan Sutton Publishing
Printed in Great Britain by
Dotesios Printers Limited

CONTENTS

IN THE DAYS when tradesmen plied their trade in the Selkirk streets, a milkman and bread boy are caught by the camera in the Kirk Wynd, 1900.

INTRODUCTION

The County of Selkirk is situated in the Scottish Borders midway between Edinburgh and Carlisle. It is a Scottish shire of great variety ranging from rolling hills to scenic rivers, valleys and woodlands. It was known in the early years of Scottish history as Ettrick Forest. Bounded to the north by Peeblesshire and Midlothian, east and south by Roxburghshire and by Dumfriesshire to the south-west, the county is landlocked almost in the centre in the Borders.

Although the County of Selkirk is only 28 miles at its greatest length and 22 miles in breadth, with many high hills and narrow valleys, it has a very successful farming community which specializes predominantly in the breeding of Cheviot and Black-faced sheep. There is some cultivation but this is mainly winter feed for the sheep and cattle which graze the hills in large numbers.

The county boundary is extremely irregular and follows approximately the diagonal line of the area's main rivers, the Ettrick and Yarrow. The two rivers flow in parallel valleys until they meet at Carterhaugh, then they flow as the Ettrick Water past Selkirk and join the Tweed near Sunderland Hall. The Yarrow rises in the south-west corner of the county and flows through the Loch of the Lowes and St Mary's Loch. It then courses through the 'Dowie Dens' of Yarrow, the inspiration for many scenes of historical and romantic interest. The Ettrick, also praised in Scottish verse and song, follows a much more rugged path, through wild scenery near its source to gentle parklands where it joins the Tweed. Gala Water, only flowing through Selkirkshire for about five miles, is extremely important to the town of Galashiels through which it flows before joining the River Tweed. The River Tweed, the main Border river, passes through the county for a distance of ten miles on the eastern boundary, with the course of the Ale Water scribing a similar path in the south.

A large number of the lochs in Selkirkshire are small and some are almost inaccessible to all but the most enthusiastic walker and fisherman. The best known is St Mary's Loch, a popular beauty spot in the Yarrow Valley. Although the loch is only three miles long and less than one mile wide, (it is reputed to be as deep as the surrounding hills are high), its setting is strikingly solitary and Hogg, Scott and Wordsworth all celebrated its beauty in prose. Cauldshiels Loch, at the opposite end of the county, is also very beautiful and the Haining Loch, near Selkirk, was formerly the chief supply of water to the town.

The seat of local government was the Royal Burgh of Selkirk, the county town, whose history stretches back to when it was granted it's Burgh status in the twelfth century by King David who used Selkirk Castle as a base when hunting in the Royal Forest of Ettrick. Selkirk is situated at the eastern end of the county on the south side of the River Ettrick. It is built on a hillside as defence against marauding reivers and English raiders and was destroyed and rebuilt many times over the years.

The residents of the old town were often called to arms to defend their country, no more so than in 1513 at Flodden Field. Eighty men left the town to fight for King and Country; only one returned, with a captured English banner. This tragic episode in the town's past is re-enacted each year in the moving ceremony of the Casting of the Colours at Selkirk Common Riding. The sad ballad *The Flowers of the Forest* also refers to the desolation caused to the Borders, not only by Flodden but also by two World Wars.

The people born in the town are known as 'Souters', the ancient name for shoemakers, a trade for which the town was famed. Indeed, the town's tradesmen supplied Bonnie Prince Charlie's army with shoes during the '45 Rebellion.

With the advent of the Industrial Revolution the trade of the town changed to the production of tweed, a woven cloth made from the fleece of the local sheep, the mills being run by wheels driven by the plentiful supply of water from the River Ettrick.

The River Gala was also used to drive the mill wheels of the sister town of Galashiels, which is located some six miles from Selkirk at the eastern extremity of the county. Galashiels is a more modern town than Selkirk and, since the re-organization of local government, has become the centre of local administration and commerce. It is a much larger town, with a population of more than 12,000, while its older neighbour, Selkirk, houses 5,500 souls. The name of the town is derived from the river and the 'shielings', the Scots name for shepherd's huts, which represented the small village sited in what is now known as the 'old town'. Galashiels has no identified history apart from the development of its manufacturing industry and, although mills are mentioned in earlier times, it was not until the mid-1800s, when large factories were constructed on the banks of the Gala Water, that the town became established and prospered. The modern town owes its origins, as well as its prosperity and growth, to the enterprise of the entrepreneurs of the nineteenth century who seized the initiative and brought the tweed industry into being.

When the Industrial Revolution took spinning and handloom weaving from the cottages into the factories, Galashiels' manufacturers were first to grasp the new technologies and the town prospered in great leaps and bounds, especially when the railway was opened in 1849 to connect the Borders with the north, and later with the south. Galashiels was the county's only main-line station. Selkirk had its own branch line, connecting with the North British Railway at Galafoot Junction. The Waverly Route, as the line from Edinburgh to Carlisle was called, closed under the Beeching Act in 1969.

The towns prospered greatly in the late nineteenth century and many large mansions were constructed, together with great improvements to the housing stock and environment. The two towns expanded as cottages and houses were built to house the influx of mill-workers from the country. This expansion continued into this century when the County and Town Councils erected many local authority houses. However, although the number of houses increased, the population of the county remained reasonably static.

A decline in recent years in the world trade for textiles has meant that the tweed industry in the county is now a shadow of its former self but has been replaced by the new technological industries associated with printed circuit-board manufacture and electronics.

Galashiels and Selkirk act as service outlets to the many farming and village communities with buses and tradesmen's vehicles plying their trade up the long county valleys. Some villages are large but compact, others straggle along the valleys, but all have a thriving family spirit with religious, educational and sporting activities extremely well supported. Clovenfords, near Galashiels, is on the road and old rail-link to Peebles. Ettrickbridge End and the village of Ettrick stand in the valley of Ettrick Water, with Yarrowford, Yarrowfues and Cappercleuch ranging up the Yarrow. Ashkirk, beside the Ale Water, is midway between Selkirk and Hawick.

In a similar manner to the changes of employment in the towns, the country people have moved from the land and cottage industries into the factories in the towns, leaving cottages to the ravages of wind and weather.

The manufacture of woollen goods was the most important industry in Selkirkshire and its development was largely due to sheep being the main livestock bred in the county. Sheep-farming is, therefore, the main agricultural industry of the county and is highly developed. The main breeds of sheep are the Cheviot, highly valued for its wool, and the Black-faced. The trade of Selkirkshire consists of the sale and export of sheep, lambs, wool and manufactured goods from its factories.

The demise of the horse in favour of the internal combustion engine in agriculture has caused a severe depopulation in the county and, in present times, the planting of pine forests over the Selkirkshire hills has reduced the farming lands considerably.

The Ettrick Forest of King David's time encompassed a vast tract of Selkirkshire, covering all the valleys with hardwood trees, and provided a hunting ground for the Scottish nobility. Lands were gifted by the King to his supporters and they built many defensive towers and keeps to protect their possessions. Romance and rivalry, power and intrigue, concerning the lords, noblemen and common people of the county, became the norm in the Middle Ages and from these times the many poets, authors and artists associated with the area took their inspirational themes. The most famous, Sir Walter Scott, although a resident of Selkirkshire for only a short time, was Sheriff of Selkirk in the 1800s and was instrumental, through his novels, in bringing about an awareness of the colourful historical panorama of Borders and Selkirkshire history. James Hogg, the Ettrick Shepherd and poet, was born in the Ettrick Valley and was a close friend and contemporary of Sir Walter Scott. William Wordsworth visited the county three times and was guided on his tours by Sir Walter Scott and James Hogg. Tom Scott RSA, the artist, and Tom Clapperton, sculptor, used different disciplines to display their artistic talent in their sensitive portrayal of the Borderland.

The artisans of the county used the brush and pen to illustrate the spirit of the Borders but the art form of photography opened its lenses to a new 'moment in time' process. Many companies have produced photographs of the county but the collection in this book is unique. All the pictures reproduced are produced from the two photographic studios opened in Selkirk and Galashiels by two Galashiels brothers, Robert and John Clapperton.

John Clapperton worked in Galashiels. His studio and business only lasted for his lifetime, though the Robert Clapperton Studio in Selkirk is still in existence, now being run by the fourth generation of the same family. All the photographs reproduced in this book have been taken by the following members of the Clapperton dynasty: Robert Clapperton (1832–1918), John Clapperton (1855–1939), William Mitchell (1869–1942) and William McLean Mitchell (1899–1986). A large proportion of the photographs are produced from the original negatives, the rest being copied from postcards and prints which have emanated from the two studios.

Royal Burgh of Selkirk

THIS PHOTOGRAPH well illustrates how the town of Selkirk is built on the side of a hill. The mansions in the foreground are Manorhill and The Firs.

A UNIQUE VIEW of the mill chimneys of Selkirk, framed by an arch of the Stane Brig. This bridge was built over the River Ettrick in 1777 and destroyed by flood water in October 1977.

A WOODEN FOOTBRIDGE crossed the River Ettrick opposite Sim's Mill to connect North and South Bridge streets, Selkirk. Corbie Lynn Mill and Cannon Street can be seen over the river.

THE OLD CAULD AT SELKIRK was used to divert the River Ettrick into a mill lade, thus providing water power to drive the tweed mills of the town.

THE COUNTY COURT BUILDINGS and St Mary's Parish Church dominate the Selkirk skyline above the Forest Road and Glebe Terrace houses.

HANDYSIDE RITCHIE'S MONUMENT TO SIR WALTER SCOTT stands in Selkirk Market Place and was erected by the gentlemen of the county in 1839. Town gas was provided by the Selkirk Gas Company for the sturdy street lamps.

SELKIRK MARKET PLACE as seen from the West Port, with the Pant Well in the foreground and, behind, the old Sheriff Court where Sir Walter Scott ('The Shirra') dispensed justice in the early 1800s.

THIS PHOTOGRAPH shows an 1870 scene in Selkirk Market Place, with the William Mills Inn (Fleece Hotel) on the right. The building in the middle is the British Linen Bank which was demolished shortly after the photograph was taken and replaced by a new bank building.

A LARGE GROUP OF TOWNSPEOPLE stand for the photographer in Selkirk Market Place in the 1920s.

THE KING'S BODYGUARD IN SCOTLAND, The Royal Company of Archers, march in procession with Selkirk Town Council through the Haining Estate to shoot for the Selkirk Silver Arrow.

KIRK WYND, looking up towards Castle Street. The entrance to the Auld Parish Kirk was by the lamp and all the houses on the right were demolished shortly after this photograph was taken in 1880.

CASTLE STREET, in the oldest part of Selkirk, leads, as the name implies, to the site of the castle. Nothing now remains of the earth and timber construction and the pele tower, or the houses which were demolished and replaced in the 1960s.

THE MEDIEVAL BURGH OF SELKIRK was defended by gates and the road to the south was protected by the South (or Foulbridge) Port. This photograph of South Port in 1900 was taken well after all parts of the gate had been removed.

SELKIRK HIGH STREET houses some of the main shops of the town, most of which are family businesses. A rare feature to present-day eyes is the Temperance Hotel on the left. The dominant spire is that of the Lawson Memorial Church.

STANDING AT THE EASTERN END OF SELKIRK HIGH STREET is a fine statue to Mungo Park, the African explorer. The photograph, taken in 1860 using a stereo camera, shows the thatched cottages at the foot of the Back Row.

A GROUP OF CHILDREN with some of their mothers stand in Curror Street, Selkirk. Behind them on the left can be seen the perimeter wall of Knowepark School.

THE HOUSES OF RAEBURN MEADOW are pictured from Spion Kop, so named as a legacy to Selkirk men's involvement in the Boer War. All the fields between the houses and Curror Street (at the top of the picture) are now streets of local authority housing.

ALL THAT REMAINS of the old Selkirk Parish Kirk are the outside walls and a reconstructed bell tower. It was here that William Wallace was proclaimed Guardian of Scotland in 1297.

A NUMBER OF FRENCH PRISONERS were billeted in Selkirk during the Napoleonic War and were allowed to walk no further than this small tree, which is to be found on the Bridgelands Road.

SENIOR BURGH OFFICER JIMMY DOUGLAS 'Crying the Burley' in Selkirk's West Port.

THE ROYAL BURGH STANDARD BEARER for 1907, George Downie, receiving his Sash of Office from Mrs Robert Sim on Selkirk Common Riding Morning, in front of the Victoria Hall.

ROYAL BURGH OF SELKIRK STANDARD BEARER George Mitchell, on Seagull, galloping in at Selkirk Toll after Riding the Marches in 1956.

A CRAFT STANDARD BEARER of 1899 casting his Incorporation's flag in the time-honoured manner. Selkirk Market Place is crowded every year for this moving tribute to the Battle of Flodden.

SECTION TWO

Selkirk to Galashiels

A MILKMAN threading a careful path through the flood waters on the Selkirk–Galashiels road near Bridgeheugh, watched by an anxious pedestrian.

RIVER AND FIELDS merge under the waters of the River Ettrick to flood Lindean Smiddy and cottages as seen from Lindean Bridge.

THE MANSION OF SUNDERLAND HALL, near Lindean, stands in beautiful parklands between the rivers Ettrick and Tweed.

THE MEETING of the River Tweed with its tributary, the Ettrick Water, takes place three miles downstream from the county town of Selkirk. The railway viaduct which spanned the Tweed at this point carried the Galashiels–Selkirk branch line and has now been replaced by a modern road bridge.

A LADY CYCLIST passes the old Toll House at the Galashiels end of the Tweed Bridge on her way to Selkirk, with the Rink Road leading away to the right.

CASCADE HOUSE nestling among its well-wooded garden with, above and in the distance, Hollybush Farm and cottages standing on the old road to Galashiels.

BOLESIDE STATION, on the Selkirk–Galashiels branch line, with Faldonside House in the foreground and Glenmayne House above.

BOLESIDE HOUSE, a Victorian mansion, was converted into an old people's home in November 1950. It was the first of its kind in the Borders and was opened by Mr John Mann, Convenor of Lanarkshire County Council.

THE RIVER TWEED overflowing its banks at Glenmayne Haugh, near Boleside, has curtailed the stroll of Galashiels' ex-Provost William Rutherford. The Haugh was leased from Gala Estate by Galashiels Town Council in 1936 as a recreational area.

A PASSENGER TRAIN TO SELKIRK, pictured at Galafoot Junction in 1906. The branch line to Selkirk opened in 1854, following the valleys of the rivers Tweed and Ettrick.

SECTION THREE

Burgh of Galashiels

THE BORDER WARRIOR. A bronze equestrian statue in front of the War Memorial clock-tower in Galashiels, the work of Thomas J. Clapperton, son of John Clapperton, photographer.

THE SHOPS AND BUILDINGS shown in this 1906 view of Bank Street are almost unchanged and are now complemented by formal gardens opposite. The mill buildings shown at the far end of the street were known as Walkmillhead and were demolished in the late 1940s.

THE VOLUNTEERS' HALL, Galashiels, was built in 1874 at a cost of £3,500. In the gardens next to the hall were tomato houses owned by Mr Yellowlees.

THE AULD CORN MILL was demolished in the early 1900s and the foundations were used in the construction of the fountain. The carts belong to Galashiels Town Council.

THE BURGH CHAMBER, as seen from Bank Street, was built in 1867 and enlarged in the early 1920s with the addition of the War Memorial clock-tower. This was unveiled by Field Marshal Earl Haig of Bemersyde on Sunday, 4 October 1925.

MARKET STREET is overlooked by the Gothic Roman Catholic Church of Our Lady and St Andrew. The building on the left was owned by Mr Watson, drysalter.

ABBOTSFORD ROAD looking towards the Gala Aisle in the Old Burial Grounds of Galashiels.

FROM THE 1920s, Galashiels Town Council allowed the Market Square to be used as a parking place for buses. The building with the small clock-tower is the former Corn Exchange and facing this was Mitchell's blacksmith's shop.

AN EARLY PHOTOGRAPH of Galashiels Market Square looking towards the Burgh Chambers. The King's Temperance Hotel was partly demolished when the street was widened, though half of the building remains.

OVERHAUGH STREET pictured in 1905 is virtually unchanged today.

THE JUNCTION of Galapark Road and St Andrew's Street show little change today from when this photograph was taken in 1905.

THE ELEGANT VILLAS AND HOUSES of Scott Crescent lead towards St Paul's Church. The entrance to Gala policies, now the Scott Park, is on the right.

OLD GALA HOUSE, the oldest house in Galashiels, is the former residence of the Scotts of Gala and the Pringles before them. Its oldest part dates from the second half of the sixteenth century.

THE LACK OF TRAFFIC allowed the photographer to arrange this large group at High Buckholmside – impossible now, as this road is part of the main A7 trunk road to Edinburgh.

GLENDINNING TERRACE SCHOOL was built by Melrose School Board in 1876, rebuilt in 1936 and is still in use as a Primary School.

STANDING BESIDE THE OLD ROAD from Galashiels to Lauder is Heatheryett smallholding. The fields behind are where the Ladhope Golf Course is now located.

THE PRINCIPALS AND SUPPORTERS of the first Braw Lads Gathering pose for the camera at Torwoodlee Tower in 1930.

A MOUNTED POLICE ESCORT for the Braw Lad and Lass on the Selkirk road at Brunswickhill on their return from Abbotsford.

DURING THE 1934 visit to New Gala House, Provost Hayward toasts Braw Lad Walter T. Brydon and Braw Lass Jean S. Allan with (on the right) Mr J. Scott, the Laird of Gala, and Mr D. Stalker (on the left).

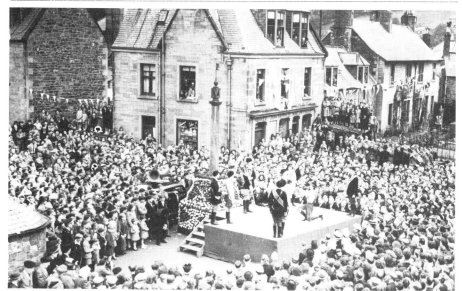

THE ROSES CEREMONY of the Braw Lads Gathering being enacted at Galashiels Old Town Cross in 1961. Braw Lad was A. Scott Amos and the Braw Lass was Irene Laidlaw.

THE GALA DAY SPORTS in progress at Raid Stane Haugh, Galashiels. In the background (right) are the electricity generating station of the Galashiels Electric Supply Company and Langlee House.

A HORSEMAN walks his pair of Clydesdales on a snowy Hollybush Road, near the Seven Trees at Galashiels.

SECTION FOUR

The Tweed Valley

THE RINK FARMHOUSE AND STEADINGS hide under a mantle of snow. Near the farm is the oldest settlement in the county. Relics from this site date from the second century AD.

THE TWEED VALLEY, framed by the trees of the Rink Road, has been a popular view for artists and photographers over many years.

THE RUIN OF THE OLD HOUSE OF FAIRNILEE, the seat of the Ker family, stands on a terrace below the modern mansion on the banks of the River Tweed above Yair Bridge. It was here that Alison Rutherford wrote the tragic ballad, *The Flowers of the Forest*.

FAIRNILEE HOUSE stands in magnificent formal gardens in the Tweed valley near the Yair Bridge. The garden boasted a beautiful ornamental terrace.

THE VILLAGE OF CLOVENFORDS photographed in the early 1900s from the road leading to the school and church at Caddonfoot.

AT THE TURN OF THE CENTURY the Tweed Vineries at Clovenfords, heated by five miles of hot-water pipes, yielded nearly 15,000 lb of grapes.

THE SMALL VILLAGE OF CLOVENFORDS stands astride the road from Galashiels to Peebles and had a station on the former North British Railway branch line.

CLOVENFORDS HOTEL was frequently visited by Sir Walter Scott when fishing and, in 1803, William Wordsworth and his sister Dorothy stayed for one night. Outside stands a fine statue of Sir Walter.

MEMBERS OF THE CONGREGATION leaving Caddonfoot Church while a christening party chat to the minister, the Revd D. MacCuish.

THE HALL was presented to the people of Caddonfoot by Lady Anderson of the Yair in 1930.

ASHIESTEEL BRIDGE (or Low Peel Bridge) over the River Tweed was reputed to be the longest single-span bridge of its type when built in 1847.

PEEL HOUSE AND GROUNDS were converted into a military hospital during the Second World War and afterwards became the hospital serving the Scottish Borders. The hospital has only recently been replaced by the building of the Borders General Hospital near Melrose.

THE MANSION OF ASHIESTEEL was the residence of Sir Walter Scott for eight years. During this period he wrote *The Lay of the Last Minstrel*, *The Lady of the Lake* and *Marmion*, plus part of *Waverley*.

THE RIVER TWEED at this point, near to Elibank, acts as the county boundary with Peeblesshire. The photographer's means of transport was his bicycle.

ELIBANK TOWER, somewhat derelict now, was the home of Sir Gideon Murray and his daughter, Agnes (Muckle-mou'ed Meg) in the early seventeenth century.

ELIBANK HOUSE stands in the last vestiges of the old oak Forest of Ettrick which covered vast tracts of the county.

One of the most attractive country seats in Selkirkshire is Yair House built in 1788 by Alexander Pringle. The beautiful Georgian mansion stands beside a quiet stretch of the River Tweed and is a building of architectural merit.

THE THREE-ARCHED YAIR BRIDGE spans the River Tweed carrying the narrow carriageway of the Selkirk to Peebles road.

The Yarrow Valley

NEWARK TOWER, ancestral home of the Scott's, stands proud by the flowing waters of the Yarrow.

THE MONUMENT erected by Sir John Murray to the memory of the Covenanters who fought and fell at the Battle of Philiphaugh in 1645.

THE SCOTT PLUMMER FOX HOUNDS (now called the Lauderdale Hunt) leaving Philiphaugh House in the early part of the century.

STANDING ABOVE THE RIVER YARROW in a beautiful wooded setting, Harewoodglen House was built as the dower house for the Dowager Lady Murray in around 1850.

AT FOULSHIELS IN THE YARROW VALLEY is the ruined cottage which was the birthplace of Mungo Park, the African explorer.

BROADMEADOW YOUTH HOSTEL, the first Scottish centre, was opened in May 1931. The Warden was Miss Anderson and the hostel catered for 30 people.

A GROUP OF DIGNITARIES AND REPORTERS relaxing after the opening of the Broadmeadows Youth Hostel by Lord Salveson in May 1931.

THE MODERN MANSION OF BROADMEADOWS was built in the 1850s and was converted into an elegant country house hotel, gaining popularity with the advent of the motor car.

BROADMEADOWS HOUSE, hidden by the trees, is beautifully situated in formal grounds and parks.

THE BLACKSMITH OF YARROWFORD stands at his smiddy, together with the residents of the cottages. All the buildings shown have now disappeared.

THE SMALL VILLAGE OF YARROWFORD pictured from above the Gamekeeper's Cottage in Black Andrew Woods.

AN EARLY PHOTOGRAPH OF YARROWFORD showing the horse-man standing in the road in front of the village school.

THE DROVE ROAD from Traquair in the Tweed Valley climbs over the hills into the Yarrow, and here descends into Yarrowford.

THE MODERN MANSION OF HANGINGSHAW replaced an older house which was burnt down at the close of the eighteenth century. The grounds feature a unique long garden terrace.

DEUCHAR MILL was driven by the waters of the Yarrow which were diverted by a cauld upstream from the buildings.

THE HORSE AND TRAP shown in the picture are the means of transport for the photographer, William Mitchell, to allow him to transport his cameras. In the trap are his wife, Davina, and sons, Robert and William.

DEUCHAR BRIDGE was erected in the mid-1600s. It was damaged by a great flood in 1734 when the south arch was washed away and, though the replacement arch was used for a further century, when this collapsed, the bridge was left to its fate.

A PLOUGHING MATCH in progress in the Yarrow Valley near Yarrow Kirk. There are 20 pairs of horses competing, giving an excellent example of how many working horses there were in small country communities.

THE OLD KIRK OF YARROW was built in 1640 to replace the Parish Church of St Mary of the Lowes. The main items of interest are the bell, the sundial and the two south doorways. The inscription above the sundial reads – 'Watch and Pray, Time is Short.'

THE KIRK OF YARROW was completely destroyed by a fire in 1922 with only the bare walls being spared. It was re-opened the following year after considerable repairs and the photograph shows the fine interior of the church.

MITCHELL'S POST BUS appears to be parked rather haphazardly across the Yarrow road in front of the valley 'Warriors' Rest' War Memorial. Driver Jimmy 'The Post' Fordyce stands proudly in front of the Chevrolet bus.

YARROWFUES is a straggling village which takes its name from the apportioning of land (or fues) to craftsmen in an attempt to bring practical aid to the farming community. Illustrated are the village post office and hall.

THE YARROW MAIL COACH rests beside the Post Office at Yarrowfues in the early 1900s.

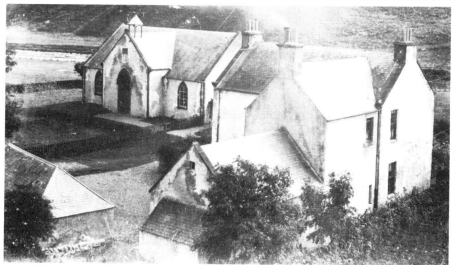

ST MARY'S CHURCH AND MANSE were erected by members of the Free Church at Yarrowfues in 1845. The first pastor, the Revd Thomas M'Crindle, ministered to the people here for 40 years.

ONE OF THE MANY HAZARDS which affect the valley motorist is the severe snowstorms which can blow up suddenly. Two men have come to assist photographer William McLean Mitchell who was caught by one such storm at Yarrowfues.

THE YARROW.

A SCOTS PINE stands proud beside the untarred farm road to Sundhope.

THE 'DOWIE DENS' OF YARROW. Famed in Border ballad and verse, seen here shrouded in snow.

LOOKING FROM THE BRIDGE over the Yarrow at the Gordon Arms, to Mountbenger School and the upper Yarrow hills. The school was opened by James Hogg, the Ettrick Shepherd, when he tenanted Mountbenger Farm.

THE HOSTELRY OF THE GORDON ARMS stands astride the Selkirk–Moffat road at its junction with the roads to Innerleithen and Ettrick. The inn was the last meeting place between Sir Walter Scott and James Hogg, the Ettrick Shepherd, in 1830.

THE POST BUS stands beside the Gordon Arms Hotel on the Paddy Slacks road to Innerleithen.

THE PASTORAL FARM OF MOUNTBENGER, once farmed by James Hogg, the Ettrick Shepherd, stands in a most beautiful part of the Yarrow valley.

THE BLANKET PREACHING, a yearly event in midsummer, is held in the abandoned burial grounds of the Parish Church of St Mary of the Lowes. The church was situated in a beautiful setting overlooking St Mary's Loch.

AN EARLY PHOTOGRAPH of the small settlement of Cappercleuch, showing the police house and church, as seen from the Selkirk–Moffat road.

CAPPERCLEUCH CHURCH was built in 1845 for the convenience of the worshippers from Meggat and outlying portions of the Moffat and Ettrick parishes.

THE UPPER REACHES of St Mary's Loch as seen from well above Cappercleuch Church. The River Meggat joins St Mary's Loch on the right.

THE OLD BRIDGE stands astride the River Meggat near to St Mary's Loch. This bridge has since been demolished and replaced by a modern equivalent, when the dangerous corners in the road were straightened.

HENDERLAND BURN flowing through the Dow Linn, near to the site of Henderland Tower, the stronghold of Cockburne, a notorious freebooter.

THE RODONO HOTEL, situated in woods above the road, overlooks St Mary's Loch and is a favourite haunt of fishermen and travellers to the lochs.

CAPPERCLEUCH POST OFFICE stands between the road and the shore, some distance up St Mary's Loch from the rest of the village.

A TRANQUIL, REFLECTIVE VIEW of St Mary's Loch with a number of sheep crossing the stream which connects the two lochs.

THE ANDREW CURRIE MONUMENT to James Hogg, the Ettrick Shepherd, was unveiled at St Marys Loch overlooking Tibbie Shiels Inn on 28 June 1860. This photograph was taken at the ceremony and is one of the earliest negatives in the Clapperton collection.

THE GLEN CAFE, near to the lochs, has satisfied the needs of the traveller from the early days of motoring.

DURING THE EXTREMELY HARD WINTER OF 1929, the Loch of the Lowes was iced over to a depth sufficient to allow local sportsmen to organize a curling match.

TIBBIE SHIELS INN sits at the meeting of the two lochs. The meetings of the district's literary greats took place in the hostelry under the stern gaze of Tibbie Shiel.

A MOTORIST AND HIS COMPANION pause above the Devil's Elbow on the Berrybush road from Ettrick to St Mary's Loch in the early '30s.

THE LOCHS nestle amid the Selkirkshire hills as seen from high up above Chapelhope and Riskinhope farms.

The Ettrick Valley

THE PRESENT ETTRICK KIRK was erected on the site of the old church in the summer of 1822. Two famous valley men buried in the kirkyard are the Revd Thomas Boston and James Hogg, the Ettrick Shepherd.

THE ETTRICK WAR MEMORIAL stands at the end of the road leading to Ettrick Kirk. It should be noted that all the floral tributes are potted plants and flowers.

STANDING IN FRONT OF ETTRICKHALL is the monument to James Hogg who was born in a thatched cottage near this spot. The monument was unveiled in 1898 by Lord Napier and Ettrick.

ONE OF THE UNFORTUNATE AFTER-EFFECTS of the Tima Flood of 1954 was the loss of valuable stock. Here the farmers load drowned sheep and cattle onto a lorry near Angecroft.

MEMBERS OF SELKIRK COUNTY COUNCIL ROADS COMMITTEE survey the substantial damage to the roads and bridges at Nether Dalgleish, upper Ettrick. The flash flood which followed torrential rains in 1954 caused severe disruption and damage to the area.

ETTRICK SCHOOL, the School House and Boston Memorial Hall stand close together under the Ettrick Hills. The hall was dedicated to the Revd Thomas Boston, minister of Ettrick Parish in the early eighteenth century.

THE POST AND TELEGRAPH OFFICE for the upper Ettrick Valley is still housed in the same building photographed here by William Mitchell in the early 1920s. The bicycle he used to travel the 18 miles to take this picture is shown leaning on the dyke.

ONE OF THE MANY PEDESTRIAN SUSPENSION BRIDGES over the River Ettrick was situated at Gamescleuch in the upper reaches of the valley.

THE OLD TOWER OF THIRLESTANE stands above the modern Mansion House, the property of Lord Napier and Ettrick. The name of the house is taken from the fact that there was a mill in the vicinity and the local tenants were 'thirled' to have their grain ground at it. The mansion has since been demolished.

A HAWKING DISPLAY being given on the hillside near Redfordgreen School. When the school closed, it was demolished and there is now no trace of its existence but for the line of Scots Pines that fringed the playground.

RANKLE BURN joins the River Ettrick near to Cacrabank Mansion and Farm, with the road to Roberton and Hawick winding its way up the valley beside the stream.

THE RUINS OF TUSHIELAW TOWER stand above a badly flooded Ettrick Valley. From this tower the infamous Border Reiver, Adam Scott, sallied forth on his thieving forays into the Borders and the north of England, until King James V ended his marauding career in 1529.

TUSHIELAW INN stands at the junction of the Ettrick and the Roberton roads and has provided sustenance to weary travellers in the valleys for many years.

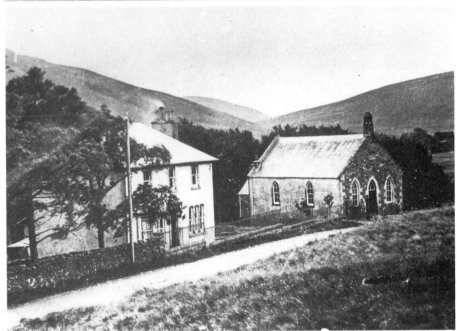

THE FREE CHURCH AT TUSHIELAW was built in 1879 and the only minister, the Revd Mr Birkett, was ordained to the charge in 1880. The substantial manse was erected a number of years later.

THE ROAD TO HYNDHOPE FARM crosses the River Ettrick on a substantial bridge. Hyndhope was a favourite rendezvous for hunting parties and has had some distinguished owners.

NEAR TO THE FARM OF ETTRICK SHAWS is a string of hill lochs which stretches in a north-easterly direction. All provide excellent fishing for keen anglers who must travel some distance for their sport.

TOWNHEAD, the last house in Ettrickbridge End, with the photographer's horse and trap waiting while he captures the scene.

ON A HILLSIDE, to the west of Ettrickbridge End, stands the Tower of Kirkhope. The old tower stands defiant and solitary above the valley, towering to a height of over 70 ft.

THE VILLAGE OF ETTRICKBRIDGE END pictured from above Cherry Dene Cottage, showing the inn, blacksmith's shop, school and parish church.

THE VILLAGE OF ETTRICKBRIDGE END pictured from the bridge from which it takes its name. The original bridge was reputed to have been built by Auld Wat of Harden when he lived at Kirkhope Tower.

CROSS KEYS INN at Ettrickbridge End is situated near the top of the village. The stairs lead to a large meeting hall which has now been converted into living accommodation.

AN EARLY PHOTOGRAPH of the thatched Post Office of Ettrickbridge End showing farm implements and, beside the lady on the left, a large beehive.

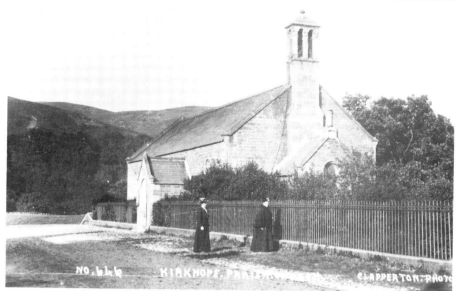

THE PARISH CHURCH OF KIRKHOPE in Ettrickbridge End was erected by the fifth Duke of Buccleuch in 1839.

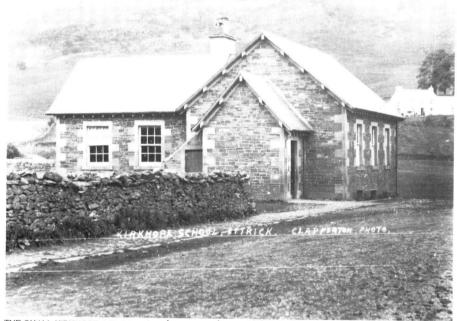

THE SMALL KIRKHOPE SCHOOL stands across the road from the parish church in Ettrickbridge End. Although it has been drastically altered in recent years, the school is still in use for primary education.

HOWFORD MILL, near to Ettrickbridge End, stands within the turn of the River Ettrick, upstream from the Brockhill Ford and suspension bridge.

IN A TRAVEL GUIDE of the late 1890s Brockhill in the Ettrick Valley is described as having 'The tidy looking, whitewashed cottages bespeaking a condition of comfort and content on the part of the fuears.'

CARTERHAUGH FARM in the Ettrick Valley was the location of a notable hand-ball match in 1815 between a team from Selkirk, Galashiels and Hawick and the men of the Ettrick and Yarrow valleys. The Selkirk team won the first match but, abandoned by the Galashiels contingent, they lost the second. The match ended abruptly in a fight.

A SHEPHERD rests with his dog on the hillside near Howden Farm, in the lower reaches of the Ettrick Valley near Selkirk.

THE ANCIENT TOWER OF OAKWOOD was built in 1602 by Robert Scott. It later became the property of Wat of Harden who married the 'Flower of Yarrow'. It is the best preserved tower in the county and is about to be made habitable again.

From Ale to Cauldshields

THE RIVER ALE rises in Roxburghshire and flows through the County of Selkirk for only a short distance. Here the stream winds its way from the hills near Castleside.

THE WOLL HOUSE stands among the trees above Ashkirk Church and school.

THE PICTURESQUE ASHKIRK PARISH CHURCH has served the residents of the village and the surrounding farms since it was built in 1791.

PART OF ASHKIRK, showing the old mill and the village hall.

A GROUP OF SOLDIERS from the Lothian and Borders Horse, photographed at their camp near Ashkirk, some time in 1914.

SYNTON HOUSE near Ashkirk, largely reconstructed in 1890, was originally built in 1777 and replaced an older house on the same site. Many parts of the older house were preserved in the new walls and these refer to a Walter Scott of the 1580s.

THE SNOW-COVERED HILLS of the Yarrow Valley, seen from the Selkirk–Lilliesleaf road at Greenhill.

A FLOCK OF CHEVIOT SHEEP grazes on the pasture in front of Whitmuir Farm House.

THE BEAUTIFUL MANSION OF WHITMUIR HALL, near Selkirk, has now been converted into holiday accommodation.

CAULDSHIELS LOCH, a secluded stretch of water among the trees, is a favourite picnicking spot, as seen here in 1905.

SECTION EIGHT

Mansions and their Staff

BOWHILL HOUSE, the residence of His Grace, the Duke of Buccleuch and Queensberry, stands in wooded policies between the Rivers Ettrick and Yarrow on the southern slope of Pernassie Hill.

BOWHILL HOUSE is famed for its beautiful furnishings and paintings. The photograph shows a small section of the Drawing Room.

BOWHILL DINING ROOM set up for a banquet. Gainsburgh's famous portrait of *Winter* is on the left.

THE DUCHESS GARDEN on the south facing terrace of Bowhill House was planned to a design of a Paisley shawl pattern.

THE DUKE OF BUCCLEUCH'S FOX HOUNDS leading off from the terrace of Bowhill House.

PHILIPHAUGH HOUSE, completely renovated in 1890 for the Strang Steel family, was originally the home of the old Selkirkshire family of Murray.

THE LARGE BODY OF BUILDERS AND TRADESMEN employed on the renovation of Philiphaugh House in 1890.

A BEAUTIFUL REFLECTIVE PHOTOGRAPH of Thirladean shows, in the foreground, an unusual view of the front of the Clapperton camera.

GARDENERS, JOINERS AND FORESTERS pose for the camera at a Selkirkshire estate in the late 1890s.

HANGINGSHAW HOUSE, which stood among fine woods and terraced gardens, was accessed by a long tree-lined drive from Yarrowford village.

THE GARDENER, BUTLER AND GAMEKEEPER seated in front of the cook and the maids at Hangingshaw House, Yarrow, 1890.

ALTHOUGH A LONG TIME EXPOSURE was required for this photograph, the gamekeeper, three curly coated retrievers and the Gordon setter have remained perfectly still.

ETTRICK SHAWS HOUSE was the property of Dr Thomas Anderson, grandson of Dr T. Anderson of Selkirk. The unique residence, standing above the River Ettrick, is constructed from iron and was built as a shooting lodge.

THE COOK AND THE MAID of Ettrick Shaws House, 1920.

THE FINE MANSION of Thirlestane House stands in its parklands near to the Ettrick road but, sadly, has now been demolished.

SHORTLY BEFORE THE HOUSE WAS DEMOLISHED, the Clapperton camera recorded the interiors for posterity and here, the hall shows its former glory.

ABBOTSVIEW, in Galashiels, was the former home of Mr Cochrane of Netherdale Mill. It was converted into a convalescent home, housing some 100 patients, by the Scottish Co-operative Wholesale Society and received residents from all over Scotland.

A VIEW OF THE DINING ROOM of Abbotsview Convalescent Home, Galashiels, in 1921.

SECTION NINE

People at Work and Play

ROBERT CLAPPERTON photographed this hunt at the Braw Gates, near Selkirk, using a stereo camera, only 25 years after the introduction of photography.

THE QUEEN'S BODYGUARD in Scotland, The Royal Company of Archers, compete for the Selkirk Silver Arrow every six years and this group of noblemen have been photographed in the Haining Estate in the late 1800s.

THIS FAMILY GROUP have been photographed in the Clapperton Daylight Studio.

A GROUP OF YOUNG PEOPLE pictured outside Kirkbrae, Selkirk, 1895.

THE TREND IN THE LATE NINETEENTH CENTURY was to have formal group photographs taken of families or friends. This group pose in a Selkirkshire garden.

AN UNKNOWN GROUP OF MEN, thought to be a football team, pose for the studio camera.

AN UNKNOWN GROUP enjoying tea in a Galashiels garden in 1920.

A LARGE GROUP OF RESIDENTS taken outside Abbotsview, Galashiels, on 20 April 1914.

A GALASHIELS FAMILY sitting in their garden in 1920.

A LOVELY STUDIO PORTRAIT of sisters Phemie and Jessie Mclean who lived near Bowland in the Gala Water valley.

THE YARROW AND ETTRICK PASTORAL SOCIETY hold an annual show in selected locations in the valleys. This photograph was taken at the Society's Show, held in 1906, at the Gordon Arms, Yarrow.

A LARGE GROUP OF COMPETITORS and spectators attending the Golf Club Gymkhana of 1923 at the first fairway on Selkirk Hill.

PLAYERS AND SPECTATORS intent on the game as Selkirk play Galashiels in the Borders Burghs Tournament, 1907, at Selkirk Bowling Green.

FINISHED in the final of the pillow fight at the Braw Lads Sports in 1934, Raid Stane Haugh, Galashiels.

THE ALL BLACKS (New Zealand Rugby Team) at Netherdale, Galashiels, in the winter of 1954 where they defeated the South of Scotland team 36 points to nil.

A HAWICK VERSUS SELKIRK TENNIS MATCH at the Municipal Tennis Courts, Selkirk, in the 1920s.

THE CURLERS OF 1929 stand for the photographer during their sport on the Loch of the Lowes with the Hogg Monument in the background.

A GROUP OF SELKIRK 'WORTHIES' curling at the Scotts Place rink in the mid 1930s. Included in the group are J. Smith, W. Mitchell, J. Grieve and D. Towns.

SELKIRK CRICKET TEAM being led out to field at Philiphaugh by their Captain, J. Grieve of Howden.

A VETERAN'S CRICKET MATCH between Galashiels and Selkirk was held in 1916.

JOHN BLAIR AND WILLIAM MITCHELL pose for this snap to show off their motor bicycles. John is on his Harley Davidson and Willie, behind, with his Indian.

PROVOST CRIGHTON AND JUDGE EDGAR stand among the Selkirk Allotment Association Members at Raeburn Meadow just after the First World War.

W. LINTON, J. BRIGGS AND G. LEITHEAD pictured in the Clapperton Studio in 1870. Briggs was the professional with Selkirk Cricket Club and was the father of the famous Johnny Briggs of England and Lancashire.

SIR JOHN N. BARRON, newly elected Liberal Member of Parliament for the Border Burghs, pictured with his wife, Lady Barron, at Galashiels in 1909.

DR ANDERSON, his wife and daughters, pictured at the front door of Ettrick Shaws House.

THE LADY OFFICERS of the Selkirk Salvation Army in 1902 were Amelia Taylor and Sarah Wilson.

THROUGH THE CENTURIES many travelling people arrived in the Borders towns and here a group of German Gypsies have been photographed at the Deer Park, Haining Estate, 1906.

THE CHARABANC, which would normally ply between Galashiels and Selkirk, has the Burgh Band as passengers to lead the fancy-dress parade around the town. It is pictured passing the gates of Selkirk's Forest Mills.

WHEN ROBERT STEWART'S ROVER SPEEDSTER CAR lost its front wheel at the Linglie, near Selkirk, a large crowd gathered to watch the Paterson brothers with their Fiat breakdown truck recover the vehicle.

DURING THE SPRING RUN OF SALMON to the spawning beds in the upper reaches of the Rivers Ettrick and Yarrow, water baillies, employed by the Tweed Commissioners, use nets to help the fish over Selkirk Cauld.

SHERIFF AIKMAN SMITH presiding over his court in the old Sheriff's Court in Selkirk in 1952. Sir Walter Scott, (the Shirra) dispensed justice in this court for 32 years until his death in 1832.

JOHN GUTHRIE, Selkirk's last Souter (Shoemaker), retired from business in 1976 after working in the trade for 52 years.

A SELKIRK POSTMAN pictured on a winter day during his rounds in Shawpark Road.

HIGHER STRETCHES of Selkirkshire roads are prone to blocking during heavy snow fall and a group of County Council roadmen have found it necessary to use a mechanical digger to clear the drifts at Smedheugh on the Selkirk to St Boswells road.

A GROUP OF SPECTATORS watches as 'wild' Ettrick lives up to its name and flows in high flood under the arches of Lindean Bridge.

THE VILLAGE BOBBY stands in the main street of Ettrickbridge End. At the turn of the century the village boasted two churches, a school, a police station and an inn.

THE 39th (HIGHLANDERS), Royal Scots marching along Scots Place, Selkirk, during the First World War.

SELKIRK'S CAULD was destroyed in 1924 and here a group of townspeople survey the damage.

SECTION TEN

The Tweed Trade

PHILIPHAUGH MILL, a Selkirk spinning mill, was driven entirely by water power using a turbine, the mill lade taking its water from Murray's Cauld. In summers when the water was low the mill was driven by a large steam engine; the use of water and steam continued until the factory closed in 1965.

THE BURN MILL IN SELKIRK was built by D. & A. Johnstone in 1871, but was destroyed by fire in the winter of 1916. Because of the treacherous condition of the roads, the fire engine which attended the scene was pulled to the mill by soldiers of the Royal Scots who were stationed in the town at that time.

ST MARY'S MILL in Selkirk, opened by Messrs Gibson and Lumgair in 1894, finally ceased to trade as a tweed mill in 1977. The buildings now house the Borders Regional Library Headquarters and also a number of manufacturing companies.

THE IMPOSING TWIN BUILDINGS OF NETHERDALE MILLS in Galashiels have dominated the surrounding area since 1873. The one on the left was used for a period by the Scottish Woollen Technical College as a production unit. This building has since been demolished but the other is still in use.

THE WOOL STORE OF ROBERT'S MILL in Selkirk is representative of similar facilities in all the tweed mills of the county. Wool store manager, Jim Douglas, and Sandy Heatlie are seen checking the quality of the wool.

WILLIE STILLIE at work on the warp mill in Forest Mill, Selkirk.

AFTER THE WOOL HAS BEEN CARDED AND SPUN, it is stored in the yarn store. Jimmy Ormiston is at work in Gardiner's Tweed Mill, Selkirk.

EX-DEACON OF THE SELKIRK INCORPORATION OF WEAVERS, Eddie Douglas is seen here at his pattern loom in Forest Mill, Selkirk, in 1950.

THE LARGEST DEPARTMENT IN ANY TWEED MILL is the power weaving shed, usually fitted out with Dobcross looms. In this picture May Sidserve is seen in Robert's Forest Mill in Selkirk.

FOLLOWING WEAVING, the wool's natural grease must be removed by a process known as milling. Jock Whitson and Tommy Robertson are seen at work in the mill house.

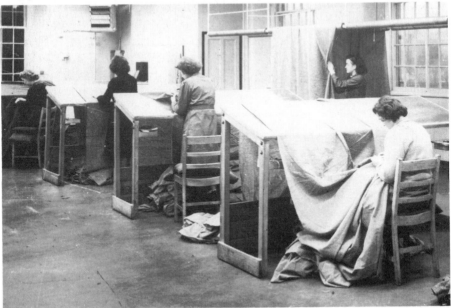

THE GREASY DARNING SECTION at the production unit of the Scottish Woollen Technical College in Netherdale Mill, Galashiels.

BROKEN THREADS, KNOTS AND OTHER FABRIC BLEMISHES in the manufactured tweed are removed by the darners. Pictured in the darning flat are, on the right, Joanne Hogg, Adeline Stott and Belle Johnstone. Gardiner's Tweed Mill, Selkirk.

DOUGLAS TAIT, seen here at the laborious but skilful job of picking.

Forestry and Agriculture

MR YELLOWLEES AND HIS MEN hauling timber from a sunlit Linglie Glen near Selkirk in 1908.

THE USE OF HEAVY HORSES was not exclusive to the farmer and here they are seen hauling timber from the woods of Hartwoodburn, near Selkirk.

DURING THE FIRST WORLD WAR women and schoolboys were employed in the woods for snedding (scrub clearing), usually under the watchful eye of a woodman. Willie Fowler is one such Selkirk lad.

SAWMILLERS working at a back-to-back bench at Hartwoodburn during the First World War. The traction engine used to drive the mill can just be discerned behind the central figure.

A LARGE GROUP OF WOODMEN AND BOYS pause for the camera outside the Hartwoodburn Sawmill.

VALLEY SHEPHERDS must tend their sheep in all weathers. Yarrow farmer Kit Watson and his collies are seen on Lewinshope Hill in typical wintry conditions.

THE FARM BONDAGER walks beside the horseman on their way to work in the Broomhill fields.

THIS YOUNG BONDAGER from Philiphaugh Farm is pictured beside the Philip Burn in 1895. Bondagers formed a female labour force which was hired by the year for extremely low pay. They were dependant on their employers for both bed and food, working outdoors in all weathers and conditions.

IN A SNOW-COVERED SHAWMOUNT FIELD, ploughing is in progress in 1925.

HERDS WERE EMPLOYED ON THE FARMS to tend the cattle and are pictured in the farmyard with young bullocks. Note the round house in the background where horses were used to drive the farm machinery.

TO SUPPLEMENT ANIMAL FEED IN THE WINTER, turnips are grown and are seen here being harvested on Bridgelands Farm.

AFTER A FIELD HAS BEEN PLOUGHED the soil must be broken up to allow the seed to be broadcast. Harrowing is a tedious and dusty procedure for both horse and man.

TWO PAIRS OF HORSES, under the control of their horsemen, hard at work rolling in the new grass on a Selkirkshire farm.

FARM-WORKERS hard at work with the hay in what is thought to be a Philiphaugh field.

THE LABOUR-INTENSIVE, WINTER JOB OF THRESHING in progress on Robert Stewart's Broad-meadows Farm in the Yarrow Valley.

A FARM WOMAN makes up the sheaves after the horse-drawn reaper has cut the corn on Shaw's Farm. The field behind is now Selkirk's Pringle Park.

AFTER THE SHEAVES HAVE BEEN MADE they are built into stooks, as they have been here, by an old farm labourer. Shaw's Farm, Selkirk, 1905.

ON A SMALL FARM, during harvesting, everyone was required to help. Mrs Hogarth and her son are at work in the stackyard of Sunderland Hall Farm.

MR ALEC STORRIE, Shepherd at Gilmanscleuch in the Ettrick Valley, resting with his Border collies.

MR TWEDDLE supervising his men during the annual clipping of his sheep at Joyce's Brae, near Selkirk.

A SHEPHERD, with his flock of Black-faced sheep, stands under the shade of the Scots Pines on Chapelhope Farm, in the upper reaches of the Yarrow Valley.

A WELL TURNED OUT HORSE AND CART being displayed at A. & R. Stewart's Lewinshope Farm in preparation for Yarrrow Show, 1910.

'Waiting for Daddy,' Bridgelands Road, Selkirk.